GIRLS GET STITCHING!

Shirley Mclauchlan

Personalize Your Clothes,
Your Room & Your Stuff
10 Embroidery Stitches, 20 Projects

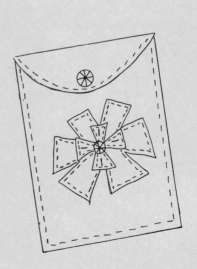

GIRLS GET STITCHING!

Shirley Mclauchlan

**Personalize Your Clothes,
Your Room & Your Stuff
10 Embroidery Stitches, 20 Projects**

Photography by Steven Wooster

FunStitch
STUDIO
stitch your art out.

Girls Get Stitching

First published in the United States in 2013
by FunStitch Studio, an imprint of
C&T Publishing, Inc.
PO Box 1456
Lafayette
CA 94549

Copyright © Berry & Bridges Ltd 2013

Designs and patterns copyright © Shirley
Mclauchlan 2013

Created and produced by
Berry & Bridges Ltd
Belsize Business Centre
258 Belsize Road
London
NW6 4BT

Designer: Darren Brant
Editor: Katie Hardwicke
Illustrations: Shirley Mclauchlan
Original concept: Ed Berry

ISBN 978-1-60705-833-5

Printed in China

CONTENTS

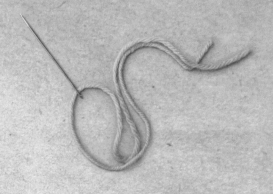

To Make For Your Home

Useful Stuff

To Give To Friends

Introduction

When I started writing this book, I thought back to my teenage years and I remembered seeing my Mom making and baking. She always had something on the go—a knitted sweater or an embroidered pillow, or just baking a cake for tea. I guess this "busy bee" approach has never left me and I really enjoy making and creating pieces of work not just for my family but also as the basis of my business.

There really isn't anything nicer than making something special for someone special. I also like the idea that I can create something individual—and never two the same. For me, the more special and individual a piece is the better. Clients give me personal details and I interpret them with stitches or symbols and a lot of help from my husband, who draws out animals and shapes. For this book I asked him to "draw me a fawn, oh, and a pair of angel wings!" We both work from home, me in my tiny studio full of yarn/thread/blankets and he in his full of paint and books. In the middle is the computer where Kitty, our teenage daughter, does her homework. Kitty was a great sounding board for this book; she liked the little fawn and she loved the lips and pompom scarf—it was her idea to put strawberries on slippers!

With my family's input (including our naughty Jack Russell, Teddy, who has a love of pink yarn!), *Girls Get Stitching* has been a great project to work on. The idea of this book is to inspire you to simply "have a go." With just a few easy embroidery stitches and a lot of imagination, you can design and decorate clothes and make personal, fun gifts. Also, in this techno-mad world, it is nice to do something practical with your hands—it allows you to have some "thinking time." The wonderful thing about embroidery is that you can put it down and go back to it later, it isn't messy, and once you have stitched something, it could last for a very long time.

How to use this book

The projects in the book will help get you started with some ideas on how to make and personalize your own clothes or accessories. You can adapt the projects as you wish and each has been broken down into different elements; you can do them all, or just part of the design, or mix in another design, it's up to you. So, you could put a strawberry on a dish towel and a cherry on a T-shirt... above all, HAVE FUN!

The embroidery stitches I use are very easy. You don't need to worry about straight lines or keeping everything too even and regular—I think it looks nicer anyway to have some variety and is more individual, too. It is fun to mix stitches together, you could even try and create your own. Just remember to explore and practice, and trust your own judgment.

The templates for the motifs on pages 120-125 are your cutting guides for the motifs. I have included more complicated stitch markings on some of the templates. For the rest, you can follow the stitching patterns shown in the photographs, or adapt the design or stitches as you wish. It is fine if yours look different from mine! Whatever you make will be made by you, and that makes it really special.

Basic Stuff

Once you know you want to stitch something special, you need to gather your fabrics, threads, and equipment, and learn how to work a few simple stitches. Get some ideas together about the colors you prefer and pin these up on a board in your room. You can stitch on solid or patterned fabric, and you can use special embroidery silks on cotton fabrics and thicker wool yarns on wool or felt ones. Take the time to practice a few stitches so you can create them easily.

Sampler

Stitches

Moodboards

Sampler

Things you need

Before you start to make any of the projects, you need to get a few bits and pieces together to stitch with. Listed below are the basics but some projects will need special materials. Each project has a list of what you need, together with tips on where to find more unusual items, so check that out before you start. It's a bit like baking: get all the ingredients ready first, then have fun mixing them up!

Sewing box or basket

It's a good idea to keep your sewing kit, fabrics, and so on, together in a little box (like an old shoe box) or a basket on a shelf in your room, so you always know where to find them. If your Mom sews she may well have some of the stuff you need, in which case you may not need to buy anything at all (check with her first!). Don't forget Grandma—she could also have a wealth of vintage fabrics and sewing supplies tucked away, not to mention being a great source of advice and encouragement, too!

Sketchbook

If you like stitching and making your own things, then keep a little sketchbook with notes and ideas. It is always great to keep a record of things that work well. Samplers are a fun way to practice stitches and can be used to decorate your sewing box afterward, too.

Bulletin board

Pin up your little practice-stitched pieces of fabrics on a board in your room. It looks nice and it also reminds you of colors and combinations of colors that work well for you. When I used to have a fashion studio, we always had a "moodboard" that we constantly looked at for inspiration. You could pin up images from magazines or postcards or little drawings that you make as you experiment with different stitching ideas.

Scissors

You need a good pair of long-bladed sharp scissors (for cutting fabric). Keep another pair for cutting card, as paper tends to blunt scissors (my Mom would go mad if she caught us using her fabric scissors on paper! At the time I didn't understand why but now I know how annoying it is when your fabric scissors are blunt!). You also need a small pair of embroidery scissors for snipping off lengths of threads and yarns.

Paper and card

You will need some plain white card to make templates, something stiff enough to draw around without bending or creasing. You will need some colored card, too, if you are going to make any of the stitched greetings cards, so buy this as and when you need it. Art and craft supply stores are great and you will find all sorts of different weights of card (medium-weight is best). You will also need a supply of tracing paper to trace the templates before transferring them to card.

Needles and pins

You will need two different types of needle: embroidery needles are best for working with cotton thread or pearl cotton embroidery floss; a yarn or darning needle with a large eye is needed for thicker, woolen threads and tapestry yarns. You will also need some general sewing needles for sewing seams by hand. Have a supply of good quality stainless steel pins to hold two fabrics together before stitching. It helps to keep everything in a needlecase (see page 88 for making your own) and you may need a thimble and pincushion, as well.

Thimble

A thimble helps to protect your finger when you push the needle through thicker fabric. It is usually made of steel or ceramic.

Marking equipment

You need a fabric marking pen to draw the outlines of your stitched shapes on fabric. These special pens are great because the mark that they make disappears when the fabric is washed, or try a fade-away pen that fades after 24–72 hours.

Measuring equipment

A tape measure is useful, as is a 12in. (30cm) long ruler.

Embroidery hoop

This device holds your fabric taut between the two parts of the hoop, which are tightened with a screw at the side. It helps you to stitch neatly as it keeps the fabric stretched and stable —you've probably seen ladies using these in costume dramas! They are available in different sizes, choose a medium-sized one that is easy to handle but large enough to contain your design.

Tape

I like to use masking tape as a guide for stitching straight lines as it can be peeled off after stitching. Double-sided tape is useful for sticking fabric to card (see page 15).

Fusible bonding web

This is a glue-backed paper that you iron on to the reverse of your fabric design, and then you can iron your fabric shape to a background fabric to keep it in place. It is useful for appliqué on fabrics that fray easily and, once the fabric is in place, you can stitch around the edge (see page 15).

Sewing basket

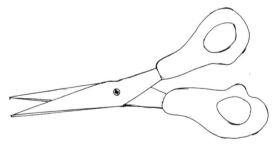

Sewing box

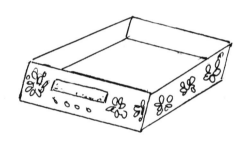

Scissors

FAR LEFT: These patterned cotton fabrics in simple checks, spots, and stripes are perfect for embroidery as you can follow the lines with your stitches. They also mix well with solid colored fabrics.

LEFT: Solid fabrics are a good base for embroidery, especially if you're working a motif, like the owl or cherries, as they will show up well on a plain background. Thicker fabrics, such as wool or felt, are ideal for working bigger stitches in woolen yarns.

TOP RIGHT: These silky threads are special embroidery silks that come in a fantastic range of colors. They work best on thin, cotton fabrics.

BOTTOM RIGHT: Wool yarns give a cozy look and create thicker stitches; they look great on wool fabrics or felt.

Fabrics

The fabrics used in the projects are all natural materials: either cotton or wool. The weights vary and some are solid, some printed. You can, of course, stitch on any fabric but working stitches on a nice fabric just adds to your enjoyment of what you are doing. You don't have to buy expensive fabrics. You can go to a thrift store and see if you can find clothes made of good fabrics, and then cut these up. I buy vintage woolen blankets and cut these up to provide base fabrics for my own embroideries. It is good to re-use.

Everyone has particular color palettes that they prefer. I like either plain, neutral colors or soft stripes and checks, and I adore polka dots and florals. Checks and stripes are very useful because they create a natural guide to stitching in straight lines!

Generally, the finer embroidery flosses work best on finer cottons and woolen yarns on thicker wools and cottons.

Threads

You will need plain cotton thread if stitching seams, and embroidery silks, such as Anchor Pearl Cotton, for embroidery stitches. You can also embroider slightly coarser stitches with wool yarn. Finer, smoother, wool yarn is generally best, such as the Anchor Tapestry yarns often used for tapestry work. Refer back to your moodboard and have fun with mixing up your threads and trying different color combinations. Remember that it is all about your taste.

Before you start stitching

Once you decide on a project you would like to make, get all the things you need together first. Look at the list at the start of the project. Read through the project steps and see what stitches are used, then turn to pages 18-19 and practice the stitches required on some scraps of fabrics, to make sure you know how to do them. Keep your samples and pin them on your bulletin board.

Transferring templates

Many of the projects have a template for the basic design and these can be found at the back of the book (see pages 120-125). You will need to enlarge the template to the right size before transferring it.

1 Place a piece of tracing paper over the design and trace the outline in pencil.

2 Turn the tracing paper over and scribble over the entire outline using a soft (4B) pencil.

3 Position the tracing paper on your card, right side up, and re-draw the original pencil line—the outline will transfer to the card beneath. Cut out the template ready to use.

Cutting out shapes in felt

1 Lay the card template on a piece of felt and draw around the outside of the shape with a fabric marking pen.

2 Once the shape is defined, cut around the outline with a sharp pair of scissors. If the project has lots of small pieces, stick them onto a piece of masking tape to keep them together.

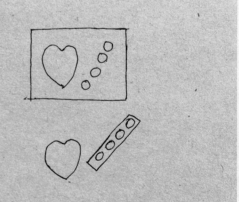

Bonding fabrics together or to card

There are different methods for bonding fabrics together or onto card and you can decide which is best suited to your project.

If your finished item is likely to be washed, then either use fusible bonding web or stitch the fabrics together. If you are attaching fabric to card, it is easier to use double-sided tape.

To stitch fabrics together

This is the most common method: simply use the stitches for the chosen design to apply the stitched fabric to the backing fabric, such as a series of running stitches outlining a motif (see page 18).

To stick fabric to card

Mark out the overall size of your design. Cut strips of double-sided tape and stick them to the card at the top, bottom, sides, and middle of the area of the design. Then lay the wrong side of the design on the sticky card, taking care to smooth it out evenly over the sticky tape.

To bond an appliqué design on fabric

Use the fusible bonding web, wrong side down on the wrong side of the appliqué fabric, and iron on the paper side of the fusible bonding web. Peel the paper backing off the bonding web and stick it to the base fabric and iron in place following the manufacturer's instructions.

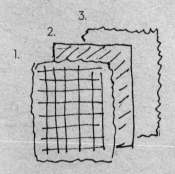

1) Top fabric
2) Fusible bonding web
3) Wrong side of backing fabric

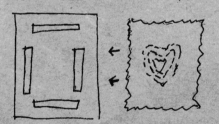

All about stitches

There are only a few stitches used in the projects, so it shouldn't be too difficult to learn them. It is a good idea to practice them first on a scrap of fabric, just so you get your hands and eyes working well together! Make sure you are sitting comfortably with a good source of light shining on the work itself. I like to listen to music when working. Remember, this is fun, so find your own way of working and enjoy the art of sewing—you are creating something that is special and made by you!

When you thread your needle, make sure the yarn is neither too long (or it will tangle) or too short, as you will have to keep re-threading the needle. Normally about 18in. (45cm) works best.

You don't need to knot one end of the yarn. Instead, learn to make a couple of tiny stitches, one on top of the other, before you start the embroidery at the beginning and just before the thread runs out at the end. This will secure the yarn without making a bulky lump on the back of the work.

When you stitch, the secret is to work in an even, regular way, trying to pick up a similar amount of fabric each time you take the needle in and out of it. My stitches are not particularly even and not always straight, so you don't have to aim for perfection, you just need to develop

a nice, easy stitching rhythm, so that you enjoy making them. It is a very personal thing and the more you do the more attuned to "your way" you will get.

The sampler (opposite) shows all the stitches in the book. You may find some stitches simpler to do than others but have a go and if you don't get it the first time don't give up—you will succeed!

RIGHT: This sampler shows rows of the stitches used in this book, from the top:
Row 1 cross stitch; row 2 backstitch; row 3 French knots; row 4 seed stitch; row 5 running stitch; row 6 single daisy stitch; row 7 couching; row 8 double cross stitch; row 9 fly stitch; row 10 lazy daisy stitch.

BELOW: With just a few stitches—backstitch, running stitch, and a few double cross stitches and French knots—you can stitch and decorate a personal message in no time!

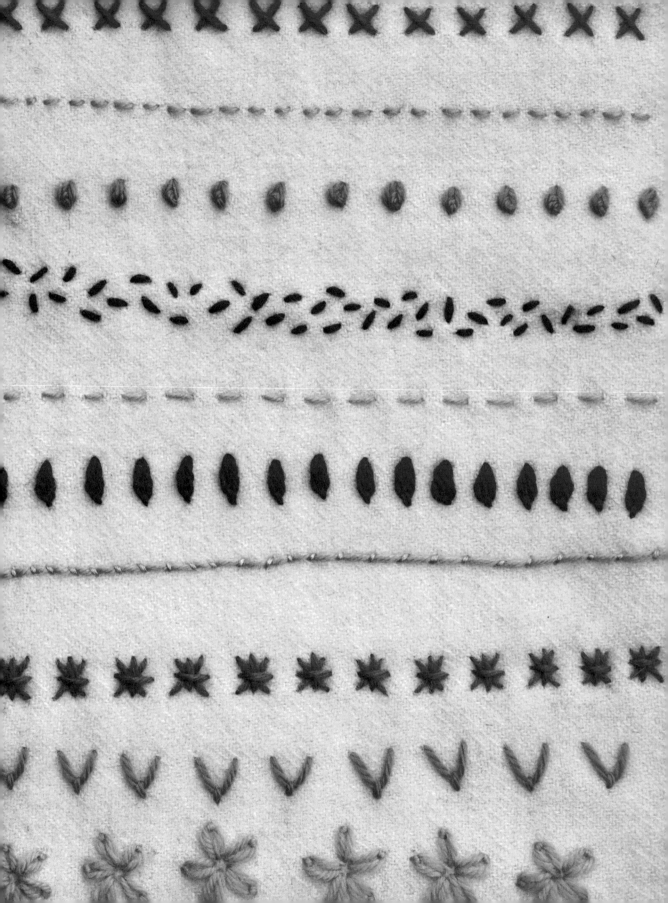

Quick guide to stitches

Cross stitch

To make one individual cross stitch, make a diagonal stitch sloping from top left to bottom right and then another diagonal stitch crossing over it from bottom left to top right, keeping the length of the stitches the same. To work a line of cross stitches, work all the bottom stitches first, then work the top stitches, bringing the needle up at the base of the bottom stitch, ready to take it down again at a diagonal top right.

French knots

These are little twists of thread made on top of each other to create a knot shape. Bring the needle through to the front of the fabric, wrap the thread around the needle tip a few times and, holding the yarn wraps with your fingertip, insert the needle back through the fabric next to it and pull the thread through to the back.

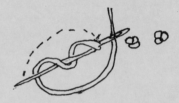

Backstitch

This looks similar to *running stitch* but you don't gather up the fabric on the needle. Instead, you take the needle backward and forward to make a line of closely spaced stitches. Bring your needle to the front, a stitch length from the start of the line. Take the needle down backward at the start of the line, then up a stitch length forward, and back down almost where you first came up. Keep working backward and forward along the line, leaving little gaps between the stitches, or joining them together to form a continuous line. If you create these stitches on a diagonal slant, starting each new stitch halfway along the previous one, this creates stem stitch.

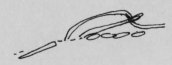

Seed stitch

This is a very easy stitch that is used to fill in areas. Make a random pattern of very small straight stitches, all the same size, scattered in different directions in the area you wish to fill.

Running stitch

This stitch is very quick and can be used on its own or combined with other stitches, such as *cross stitch*. Bring the needle up, then take it down, and bring it up again so that the stitches

are the same length. You can thread several stitches on your needle before you pull the thread through. You can make short or long stitches as you need them.

Single daisy stitch

This is a looped stitch, like *fly stitch*. To make a single daisy stitch, bring your needle up then reinsert it in the same place, leaving a small loop. Bring the needle back out with the loop beneath the needle and make a small stitch over the loop to hold it in place. If you want to make a chain, insert the needle for the next chain inside the end of the loop.

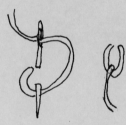

Couching

This is useful when you want to lay threads on the surface of the fabric. Create a long straight stitch to the required length and then take tiny stitches at short intervals across the thread to hold it in place.

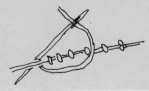

Double cross stitch

This stitch combines a normal *cross stitch* with a straight cross over the top, to produce something a little like a star. Work a cross stitch, then bring the needle up in the center between the two lower arms, make a vertical stitch, then come up to the left and make a horizontal stitch across the center, keeping all the stitches roughly the same length.

Fly stitch

Make a simple, small looped stitch and then catch the tip of the loop with another small stitch.

Lazy daisy stitch

Make a *single daisy stitch* and then create five more to form a little circle of stitches that resemble flower petals.

Moodboards

If you want to create your own colors for the projects in this book, then it will help if you do a little moodboard first, pinning your fabric choices, thread or yarn choices, and so on, onto a sheet of card or paper, and then sticking this on your bulletin board. Don't make an instant decision, but go back and look at it a few times and play with your choices before going ahead. All fashion houses use moodboards as trend information and they are a good way to test out your "look." I like to put stuff up and leave it there for a day or so before I make my decision.

RIGHT: Singing the blues—a moodboard with a predominantly cool toned palette, mixing a range of printed and solid fabrics in different weights and types.

FAR RIGHT: In the pink—a moodboard with warm tones of pink, red, mauve, and yellow, again with a range of weights and types of fabric.

To Make For You

Have fun personalizing your clothes, bags, and accessories with simple stitches and designs that will bring a quirky touch to your wardrobe. These projects use designs and motifs that you can mix and match to suit your own tastes, and, once you've made something fabulous for yourself, why not make one for your BFF, too? Perfect for a quiet afternoon of "me-time," the projects are also ideal for making with a friend, giving you lots of time to chat while you stitch.

Fawn T-shirt

Hats and gloves

Pompom scarf

Peace jacket

Mobile cozy

Rainbow tote

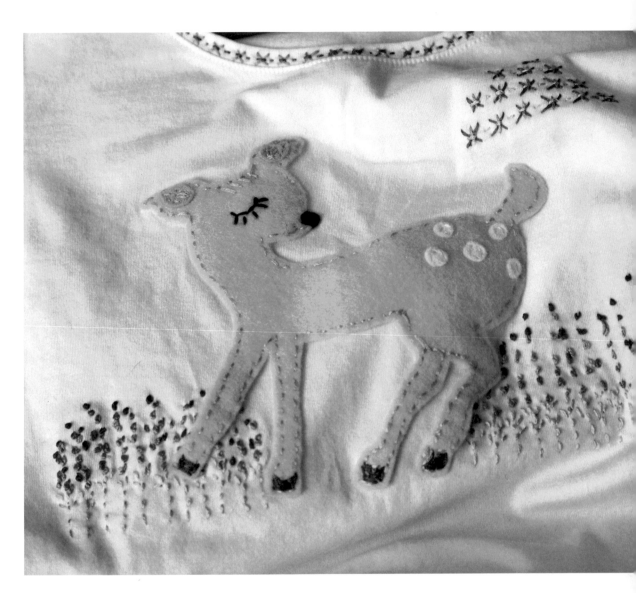

Fawn T-shirt

This sweet design is bound to be popular as it is such a nice way to make a simple white T-shirt very special. If you find the flowers surrounding the little fawn a little complicated, you could change them for a few rows of cross stitches in similar colors.

Making the fawn design

A pure cotton T-shirt is much nicer to stitch on than manmade fibers, so look out for some inexpensive pure cotton ones, if you can. As the fabric is quite stretchy, you may find it easier to use an embroidery hoop when stitching on the fabric (see page 11) as it helps to keep it taut.

Things you need

- Template on page 120
- White cotton T-shirt
- Small amount of pale pink felt
- Tiny amounts of beige and white felt
- Anchor Pearl Cotton embroidery floss in white, pale pink, dark pink, red, green, light mauve, dark mauve, and brown
- Anchor Tapestry wool yarn in black
- Embroidery needle and scissors
- Tapestry needle

Before you start

Make a template from the pattern on page 120. Trace around the template onto a piece of pink felt and cut out carefully. Cut out two small triangles of beige felt for the ears and five little white circles of felt for the spots on the fawn's back.

How to stitch the fawn design

1 Before attaching the fawn to the T-shirt, start by stitching the white circles in place on it's back, using a few white running stitches.

2 Then stitch the ears in place on the head, again using a few running stitches.

3 Pin the felt fawn in place on the T-shirt. Stitch all around the fawn outline with backstitches (see the photo on page 25). Mark the hooves with a few small straight stitches in brown.

4 Using the black wool yarn, work the fawn's eyelashes using backstitch and straight stitches, and the nose with a few straight stitches.

How to stitch the cross stitch decoration

1 Make a little pyramid of mixed running and cross stitches in three colors above the fawn's tail.

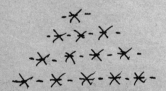

2 Add a row of running stitches in a different color along the neck border. Overlap these with cross stitches in a different color.

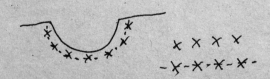

How to stitch the flower garden

1 Work the flower garden by dividing up the flowers into stems, leaves, and flower stalks. Work the green stems first using running stitches to one side of the fawn, and another set of similar stems on the other side.

3 Finally, add the flowers on each stalk using French knots. Work them one color at a time, in three colors, in a random design.

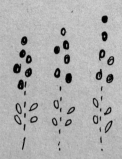

2 Add the green leaves on top of all the stems, using small seed stitches.

Other ideas

If you don't want to do quite so much stitching, you could leave out the flower garden and the extra cross stitch decoration and just stitch the fawn. You could also use just the simplified fawn decoration on a bag, if you like.

Alternatively, use one of the other animal designs, such as the fox or the owl, or a bird like the peace dove, instead of the fawn on the T-shirt.

p 76   Use the Owl or Fox motif instead of the fawn

p 66   Use the Fawn motif on a tote bag

Peace jacket

Why not personalize an old denim jacket with some cool embroidery? Here is one which has different designs for the front and the back. The front design just uses rows of stitches in different colors, while the back sports a sparkly peace symbol. You can follow these ideas or adapt them to suit your particular jacket. You could also add some embroidered buttons (see page 36) for extra decoration.

Making the peace jacket design

On the jacket front, add some simple running and cross stitches (or a combination of these) to the collar and pocket or pockets, and to the yoke seams. For the jacket back, jazz it up with a sparkly peace symbol!

Things you need

- Old denim jacket
- Paper for template and a round object, like a plate, to draw around, approx 8 in. (20cm) diameter
- Fabric marking pen
- Embroidery hoop
- Masking tape
- Anchor Pearl Cotton embroidery floss in 4 different colors, I used: turquoise, cream, pink, and dark pink
- Silver sequins
- Embroidery needle and scissors

Where to find

Pick up an old denim jacket inexpensively in a thrift store. You can buy all the sewing equipment from a fabric or notions department or craft store.

How to stitch the jacket collar

1 First, stitch around the outside of the collar with big cross stitches in one color of thread.

2 Then add running stitches in a contrasting color through the center of each cross stitch.

3 Now add a few rows of running stitches in different colors following the shape of the collar to create a funky border.

How to stitch the pocket and yoke

1 Outline the pocket tops with running stitches, following the shape of the pocket. Lift the flap to stitch across it.

2 Insert a piece of card into the pocket and decorate it with rows of cross and running stitches in different colors.

3 Add some different stitches, such as a row of French knots, on the yoke seam. You can pick out other details and seams on the jacket, if you like.

How to stitch the peace sign circle

Using an embroidery hoop (see page 11) when stitching this will help to prevent the fabric from puckering and also makes it easier to stitch neat straight rows.

1 Draw around a suitably sized plate or other round object to make a paper template. Pin the circle template to the center back of the jacket and mark out the shape.

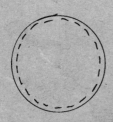

2 Insert the area of the jacket to be embroidered into the hoop. Stitch around the marked circle in running stitch using one color of thread.

3 Then add two further rows of running stitches in two different colors, following the shape of the circle.

How to stitch the inside peace sign

1 Using a strip of masking tape, position it with one edge on the center vertical line of the circle. Work the first row of running stitches next to it. Peel off the tape.

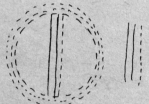

2 Stitch a further row of running stitches to each side of the first row, using different colors.

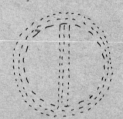

3 Next, use a strip of tape to similarly mark each side arm of the peace symbol so they meet to form a triangle.

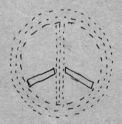

4 Mark out and stitch the side arms with three rows of running stitches as in Steps 1 and 2 above.

5 To add some sparkle, stitch sequins to the outside of the circle and the outer edges of the peace symbol.

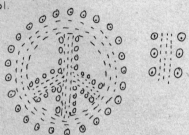

6 To attach a sequin, make a knot in the thread. Position the sequin, wrong side down, on the right side of the fabric and hold it in place. Bring the needle and thread from the wrong side of the fabric through the center of the sequin, make a stitch over one side of the sequin, and take the needle and thread to the back.

Bring the needle up through the center of the sequin again and make another stitch opposite the first stitch, taking the needle and thread to the wrong side.

Fasten off the thread (see page 16).

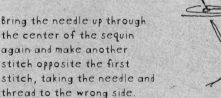

Little buttons

Sometimes you just need to make one small change to transform an outfit. Buttons are a great place to start—use a button making kit and with a few stitches you'll have something unique to add to a jacket, bag, or make into a charm.

Making the little buttons design

Either choose a solid color or a patterned fabric, add some stitches or a stitched motif, and then assemble following the button-maker instructions. Sew the button to your outfit or make lots and decorate a bag.

Things you need

- Self-cover button making kit
- Piece of solid or patterned fabric
- Fabric marking pen
- Anchor Pearl Cotton embroidery floss in different colors
- Embroidery needle and scissors

Where to find

Self-cover button making kits are available from fabric and craft stores or online. Use scraps of fabric or recycle fabric from a favorite top or dress that no longer fits. You can embroider onto printed fabric as well as solid, just pick out an area of the pattern to outline with a few stitches.

Before you start

Follow the instructions on the button making kit to cut out the fabric to the right size for your button—it usually requires a circle at least ¾in. (2cm) larger than the front of the button.

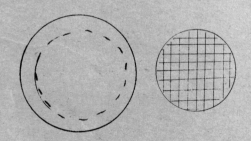

How to stitch buttons

1 Mark out a circle on the fabric for the button and then fill in this area with your chosen design, such as cross stitches, a cherry, or a peace symbol.

2 Here are two versions using cross stitches: one with double cross stitches and the other using cross stitches and running stitches.

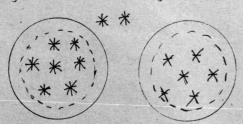

3 Try out a miniature cherry design using single daisy stitches in embroidery floss or wool thread.

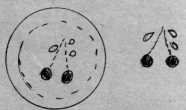

4 Or make a peace sign (see page 35) with a circle of running stitches and the central shape in stem stitch.

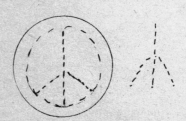

5 Following the kit instructions, add the back to the button, making sure that your design is centered, and then snap the back into place.

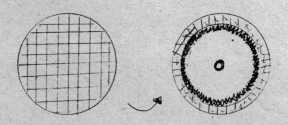

Phone cozy

This is a great idea for a gift, and is so simple that you'll want to make one for yourself, too. Choose embellishments in your favorite colors and add initials and fun motifs to make it easy to identify at the bottom of your bag.

Making the phone cozy design

Use the template to cut out the cover shape—you can make it without the flap if you like, to create a slipcase, or adjust the template to fit your cell phone. Cut out your embellishments and stitch them in place before stitching the seams.

Things you need

- Template on page 121
- Piece of felt for the cover
- Scrap pieces of felt in 3 different colors
- Scissors
- Fabric marking pen
- Anchor Pearl Cotton embroidery floss in contrasting colors, I used pink and purple
- Embroidery needle
- Snap fastener

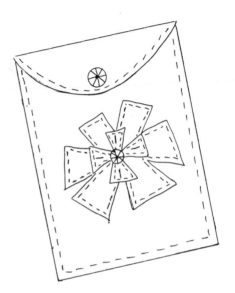

Before you start

1 Copy the template on page 121. Trace around the template onto a piece of felt and cut it out—you can cut it without the flap to make a slipcase if you like. Adapt the template to fit your phone.

2 Cut out two circles of felt in two different colors, one smaller than the other (you can draw around a button or jar lid to make a circle). Clip the edges as shown on page 90. Cut out another tiny circle in white felt for the center.

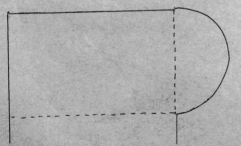

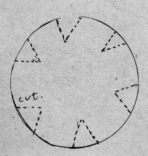

How to stitch the cozy

1 Pin the layers of your design to the front of the cozy cover. Then stitch through the center of the appliquéd layers to the cover with a double cross stitch.

2 Add running stitches to the appliquéd layers, as shown.

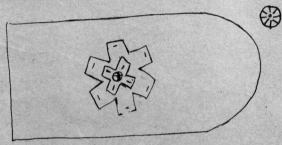 

How to make the cozy

1 Fold the cover so that your design is on the outside, then stitch the side and bottom edges together with running stitch, just in from the edge.

2 If your cover has a flap, stitch some running stitches around the edge and sew a fastener to the inside of the flap.

3 Fold the flap over and press the fastener so that it makes a mark on the outside of the pocket, then sew the corresponding fastener piece in place on the mark.

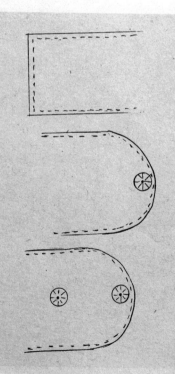

Shoe bag

This simple canvas tote bag is decorated on the front only with appliqué felt shoes, embellished with sequins, set in a circle of embroidery stitches and sequins. The top of the bag is decorated with running and cross stitches in two colors. Double cross stitches in bright pink are scattered randomly within the stitched circles.

Making the shoe bag design

You need to cut out the shapes for the shoes and stitch any decoration onto them before stitching them to the bag front, and add the rest of the embroidery stitches for the decoration.

Things you need

- Templates on page 122
- One linen, hemp, or canvas tote bag in a plain, neutral color
- Paper for template and a round object, like a plate, to draw around, approx 8in. (20cm) diameter
- Small piece each of dark pink felt and a scrap of pale pink felt
- About 50 gold sequins
- Anchor Pearl Cotton embroidery floss in bright pink, pale pink, turquoise, red, and dark red
- Fabric marking pen
- Embroidery needle and scissors

Where to find

You can find plain tote bags in craft stores, or online.

Before you start

1 Make a template from the pattern on page 122. Trace around the template onto a piece of pink felt twice and cut out the shapes neatly. If your shoe fabric has a right side, make sure you flip the template to make a matching pair.

2 Make a template for the bow shape and trace around it twice onto a piece of pale pink felt and cut out the shapes neatly.

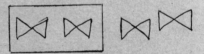

3 Stitch the bows to each shoe with running stitches. You can scatter random stitches in the bow for a pretty effect.

How to stitch the shoes

Position one shoe shape on the bag front and stitch it in place with running stitches following the design shown in the photograph on page 44. Then stitch the other shoe shape in the same way (making sure you've flipped it over so that it is facing the opposite direction).

How to add the circle

1 Make a paper circle template by drawing around something with a diameter of about 8in. (20cm)—a plate or saucepan lid work well—onto tracing paper. Position the template in the center of the bag over the shoes, and mark the circle.

2 Stitch around the circle with three rows of running stitches in different colors.

3 Finally, add a row of sequins outside the rows (see page 35), stitching them to the bag with two small backstitches in a contrasting color and scatter some double cross stitch stars around the shoes.

4 Add a few sequins to each shoe.

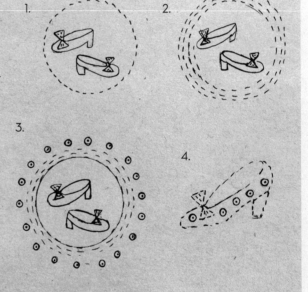

How to stitch the top

If you'd like to decorate your bag further, you could add a row of running stitches and cross stitches around the top of the bag, using two contrasting colors.

Other ideas

p 72   Use the cupcake design instead of the shoes

Hats and gloves

Plain woolen hats, scarves, and gloves can be jazzed up with some simple motifs or stitches. Here are a couple of ideas: one hat and glove set has a graphic lip design in contrasting felt on the front of the hat and the back of the gloves, the other set is decorated with XOX in running stitches on the hat front and on the back of the gloves.

Making the hat and gloves set

Start with a set of hat and gloves or mittens, ideally in a plain color but a little bit of pattern is fine, and they don't even have to match. Add a pompom in a co-ordinating color to customize your hat further.

Things you need

- Templates on page 121
- Hat and gloves
- Card

Where to find

You may have a mismatching hat and pair of gloves but by adding the same design to each you instantly make them into a co-ordinated set. Use up scraps of felt or yarn for the decoration.

For the Lips design

- Paper and pencil
- Fabric marking pen
- Felt (red or a color to match your accessories)
- Anchor Pearl Cotton embroidery floss in 2 colors, I used violet and red
- Embroidery needle and scissors
- Yarn for pompom

For the XOX design

- Paper and pencil
- Fabric marking pen
- Anchor Tapestry wool yarn in 3 colors, I used: red, cream, and mauve
- Tapestry needle and scissors

Before you start the lips design

Make a template from the pattern on page 121. Trace around the template onto a piece of felt and cut out three shapes.

How to stitch the lips design

1 Pin the lips to the front of the gloves and then stitch in place with a simple running stitch, taking care not to stitch through to the back—put a piece of card inside to help.

2 Do the same to stitch one pair of lips to the hat. You can either use the same color lips for both hat and gloves, or pick a common color to tie them all together.

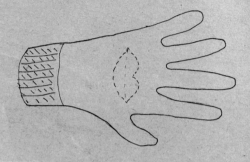

How to make the pompom

1 Decide on the size of your pompom and the color of yarn you want to use. Cut out 2 circles of card to the chosen size of your pompom. Now cut out a smaller circle in the middle of each to make a ring.

2 Put the rings together and wrap the yarn through the central hole around the rings using a tapestry needle to help feed the yarn through as the hole fills. Keep wrapping with lengths of yarn until the card ring is completely covered and the hole is nearly full of yarn.

3 Insert the tip of a pair of scissors between the card rings, then snip the yarn all around the outer edge of the ring.

4 Thread a length of yarn between the rings and tie all the pieces of yarn together. Remove the card rings to reveal your pompom. Fluff up your pompom and trim away any straggly bits of yarn. Attach to the top of the hat through the middle of the pompom.

Before you start the XOX design

Slip a piece of card inside to prevent stitching through to the back. Transfer the XOX template on page 121 to a piece of card or paper, cut out, and pin the "0" template on the hat, in the center, and mark around the template.

How to stitch the XOX design

1 Using the first yarn color, stitch around the marked shape on the hat in running stitch.

2 Change to a different color yarn and stitch a second line of running stitches, then a third in the first color.

3 Stitch the "X" with running stitch. Add a second line of stitches around the "X."

4 Do the same to stitch the "X" on the other side of the "0."

5 Repeat to add an "X" to the back of the gloves, using different colors of yarn if you like.

Pompom scarf

You can have some fun turning a plain scarf into something more individual. For this one, a rose and a leaf motif, cut from felt and decorated with stitches, have been added to the scarf ends, which have been decorated with some woolen pompoms in different colors.

Making the pompom scarf design

Choose a plain, cozy scarf in a color that works with your favorite coat or jacket and simply add a felt design to the ends. The pompoms are a fun extra if you want to add a quirky finishing touch.

Things you need

- Templates on page 122
- Plain scarf
- Paper and pencil for template
- Fabric marking pen
- Pink, red, and turquoise felt
- Anchor Pearl Cotton embroidery floss in 3 colors: red, turquoise, and dark turquoise
- Embroidery needle and scissors
- Sequins
- Yarn for pompoms in assorted colors, such as pink, orange, cream, turquoise, red, and mauve
- Card or pompom maker (optional)

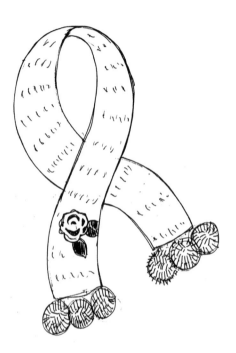

Before you start

1 Make templates from the patterns on page 122. Trace around the main rose template onto a piece of pink felt and cut out two roses, and trace around the petal shape onto red felt, and cut out ten petals for each end of the scarf, varying the size of the petal shape a little.

2 Trace around the leaf template onto a piece of turquoise felt and cut out two leaves for each end of the scarf.

How to stitch the felt rose

1 Stitch the petal shapes to each main rose using running stitch in a matching thread, using the photo on page 55 as a guide.

2 Using running stitch or backstitch, pick out the shape of the veins on each leaf.

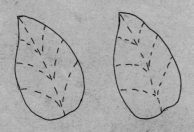

3 Place the rose shape at each end of your scarf, allowing room for a couple of leaves. Pin in place and then stitch the outlines of all three motifs in place using running stitch.

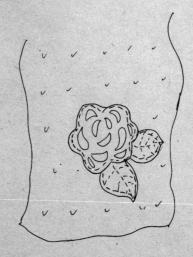

4 For a little bit of sparkle, add a few sequins around the edge of the rose, if you like (see page 35).

Other ideas

p 65   Use a few strawberries instead of the roses

How to make the pompoms

Decide on the size of your pompom and the color of yarn you want to use. Follow the instructions on page 51 amd make enough pompoms to cover the end of the scarf, then sew them in place through their middles.

Angel wings top

Made from soft felt with added sparkle, these wings will create an angelic look in no time. They look fabulous on a camisole top or T-shirt, or you could add them to a jacket or bag, or scale them down and make a festive greetings card for Christmas.

Making the angel wings top design

Use the template to cut out the wing shapes, then transform them with stitched feathers and sparkly sequins and attach them to the back of a top or jacket. You could easily adapt the design for a butterfly effect, too.

Things you need

- Template on page 123
- Camisole top or T-shirt
- Fabric marking pen
- White felt
- Anchor Pearl Cotton embroidery floss in turquoise and gray
- Silver sequins
- Embroidery needle and scissors

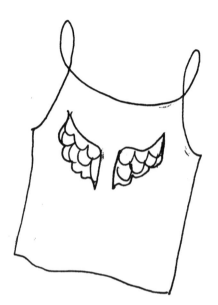

Before you start

1 Make a template from the pattern on page 123. Trace around the template onto a piece of white felt and cut out two wings, reversing the template for one wing.

2 Transfer the feather pattern from the template to the felt wings.

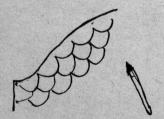

How to stitch the wings

1 Stitch the scallops of the feather pattern on each wing in running stitch, working in rows from the top of the wing down.

2 Add a sequin to the center of each feather (see page 35).

3 Pin the wings on the back of your top and stitch around the edges of each wing. Take care not to stitch through both sides of the top. If you like, insert a piece of card into the top to prevent this.

How to add the wing details

Stitch the end details to the wings with gray thread, using a few long straight stitches close together.

Other ideas

You could add the angel wings to a small purse or bag if you prefer.

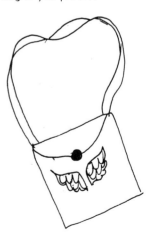

Vintage blouse

Re-invent a favorite blouse or even an old school shirt with a few pretty stitches to give it a look of vintage chic. Just a few stitches on the collar or around the sleeves will transform it into something special.

Making the vintage blouse design

This is a really quick project that gives instant results. Decide on the stitches you want to use and choose your thread colors, then just start stitching! You can keep it simple by only adding stitches to the collar, or keep stitching down the front and around the sleeves. I added a little bow tie to the blouse, too.

Things you need

- Blouse or shirt

- Anchor Pearl Cotton embroidery floss in different colors, I used: turquoise, red, green, and pink

- Embroidery needle and scissors

How to make the bow tie

1 Cut out a rectangle of fabric 5 x 4in. (12 x 10cm) and another smaller one, 2¼ x 2in. (6 x 5cm). Fold each rectangle in half as shown, with right sides together, and stitch around three sides. Turn it right side out and stitch the last side closed.

2 Put the bow together by stitching two sides of the smaller rectangle together and pushing the larger rectangle through the center.

3. Decorate the bow tie with running stitches (or cross stitches).

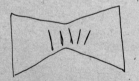

How to stitch the front

1 Open up the shirt and stitch some little groups of flowers along the button band or placket, using running stitch for the stems.

2 Then add the leaves in chain stitch.

3 Finally, add the flowers in another color using a few French knots at the top of each stem.

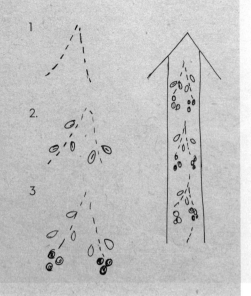

How to stitch the collar

Just a few simple running stitches can look really good. Follow the edge of the collar with a line of stitches, and repeat on the sleeve cuffs, if you like.

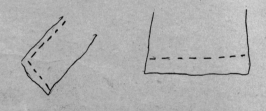

How to attach the bow tie

Attach the bow tie to the top of the button band with a small safety pin or a few stitches.

Other ideas

 p 19   For a quicker version, create rows of stitches instead of the flowers. Fly stitch would work well.

Rainbow tote

A bright and cheerful rainbow motif is perfect whatever the weather and this bag will look great with any outfit. Keep it simple with just the rainbow design, or use the colors to add extra stitching to decorate the handles and seams.

Making the rainbow tote design

Take a plain bag and trace a semicircle on the front, then follow the shape with lines of running stitch to make the rainbow. The bag would look great with a few stitched buttons, too—see page 36 for some ideas, or recycle old buttons for a boho look.

Things you need

- Paper for template and a round object, like a plate to draw around, approx 3in. (7.5cm) diameter

- Fabric marking pen

- Linen, hemp, canvas, or felted wool tote bag in a plain, neutral color

- Anchor Tapestry wool yarn in rainbow colors, such as red, yellow, pink, blue, orange, purple, green

- Tapestry needle and scissors

Where to find

You can find canvas bags at craft stores or online. The one shown here measures approx 13½ x 15½in. (34.5 x 39.5cm), plus 7in. (18cm) high handles

Before you start

1 Make a paper circle template by drawing around something with a diameter of about 3in. (7.5cm)—a small plate or saucepan lid work well. Fold the template in half.

2 Mark the semicircle on the center front of the bag.

How to stitch the rainbow

1 Use a strip of masking tape to mark the base of the rainbow to help you start and end your stitches in line. Stitch a double line of running stitches following the shape of the semicircle in the first color of the rainbow.

2 Add another double row in the next color, and continue stitching two rows of each color until the rainbow is complete—red, yellow, pink, blue, orange, purple, then green—fourteen rows in total. Remove the tape.

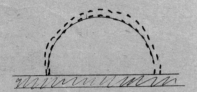

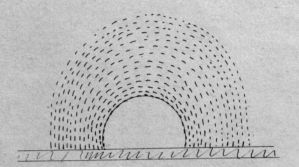

How to add decorative details

1 For extra color, stitch a row of running stitches around the top of the bag in one color. Add a second row lower down.

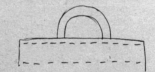

2 Next, work cross stitches through the top row of running stitches, in a contrasting color.

3 Add two rows of running stitches in different colors down the center of the handles.

To Make For Your Home

Hand-stitched homewares are always popular and there's plenty here to choose from, like cozy pillows, cute slippers, and even some fantastic kitchen accessories to make cooking even more fun! The designs can all be adapted as you wish—you could choose a theme, like the fox or strawberries, and use the motif to decorate not only a pillow and slippers, but a drawstring laundry bag too, to give your room a co-ordinated feel.

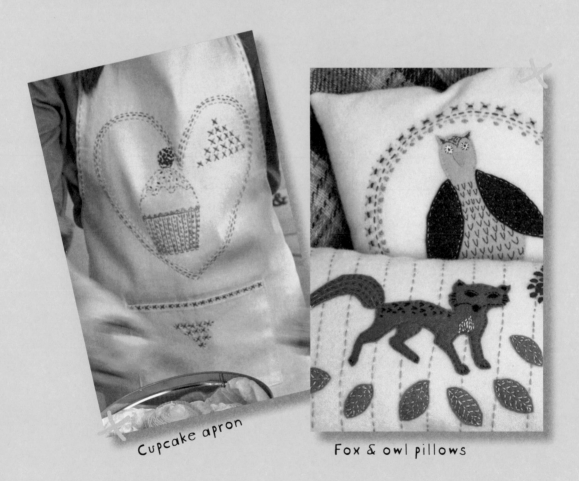

Cupcake apron

Fox & owl pillows

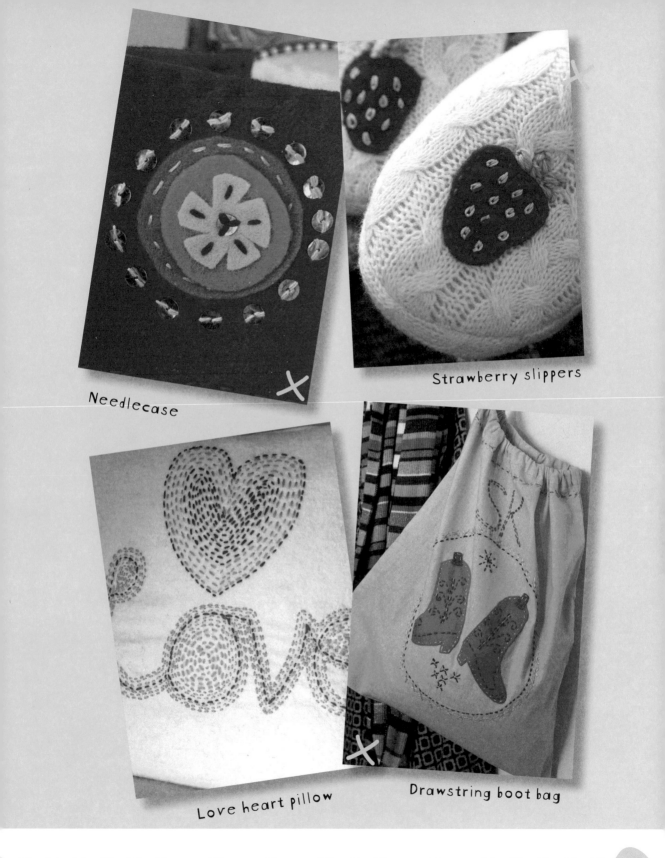

Needlecase

Strawberry slippers

Love heart pillow

Drawstring boot bag

Cupcake apron

This simple apron is decorated with a cupcake motif and a few rows of cross stitches enclosed in a heart, plus some additional stitching on the front pocket and surrounding the apron edges. You can use the entire decoration or take whatever elements you like for your own apron. The cupcake uses three different stitches: couching for the paper case, seed stitch to represent the icing, and French knots for the cherry on top. Running stitches and cross stitches are the only other stitches needed.

Making the cupcake apron design

Create your own individual decoration on a bought apron in a simple one-color fabric. The one here is a plain cream cotton pinafore-style apron, embroidered with several colors of embroidery floss.

Things you need

- Templates on page 123

- Plain cotton or linen apron

- Fabric marking pen

- Anchor Pearl Cotton embroidery floss in 8 colors, I used: pink, purple, light blue, red, turquoise, yellow, light brown, and light pink

- Embroidery needle and scissors

Before you start

Make a template from the patterns on page 123. Trace around the templates for the heart and cupcake in the positions you require on the apron. I positioned mine close to one side of the heart.

How to stitch the cupcake

1 Stitch the cupcake case with lines of couching stitches in one color (a). Add lines of running stitches inbetween (b), then create the zigzag line with stitches around the top of the cupcake case (c).

2 Outline the whole cupcake with running stitch and create a wavy line for the icing in the same stitches (d).

3 Add little seed stitches at the top in three different colors to represent sugar sprinkles (e).

4 Finally, add the cherry to the top of the cupcake, outlining a small circle in running stitches and filling it in with lots of French knots using the same color (f).

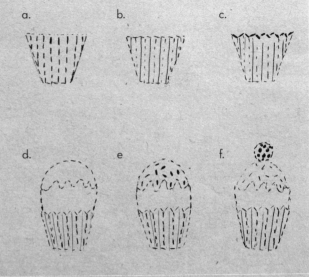

How to stitch other decorations

1 If your apron has a pocket, stitch across the top with separated cross stitches and running stitches in two colors. Fill in the center of the pocket with three or four more rows of cross stitches and running stitches in the same colors.

2 If you like, add a small pyramid of cross stitches in the heart shape using two colors.

3 Stitch around the heart outline in three rows of running stitches, each row in a different color.

4 Finally, outline the apron edge with running stitches.

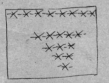

Owl & fox pillows

These two pillows have a fairly similar way of making, although both have their own instructions on the pages that follow. Both the owl and the fox are worked on a wool fabric with wool yarns, creating a lovely handmade, cozy feel to them. You could always recreate them in embroidery floss on linen, if you preferred.

Making the owl pillow

You need to trace out the template for the parts of the owl and embroider the decoration on each one, before using the outline stitches to attach the parts to the pillow front. The owl pillow measures 16in. (40cm) square and the owl himself is 8 x 6½in. (20 x 16.5cm) tall.

Things you need

- Templates on page 124
- Fabric marking pen
- Paper for template and a round object, like a plate to draw around, approx 10in. (25cm) diameter
- Small pieces of beige, brown, yellow, red, and white felt for the owl, and red and beige for the toadstool
- Anchor Pearl Cotton embroidery floss for body and toadstool
- Anchor Tapestry wool yarn in brown, yellow, rust, and white for the owl, red and yellow for the toadstool, and light and dark green and blue for the remaining decoration
- Pillowcase in plain wool, 16in. (40cm) square
- Tapestry needle and scissors

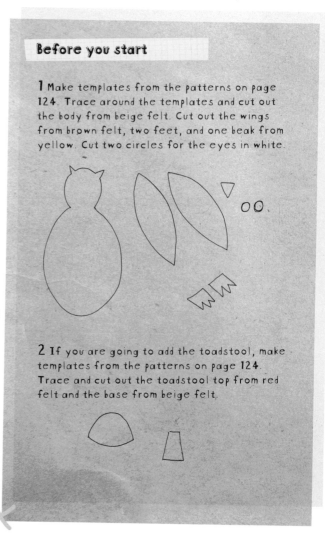

Before you start

1 Make templates from the patterns on page 124. Trace around the templates and cut out the body from beige felt. Cut out the wings from brown felt, two feet, and one beak from yellow. Cut two circles for the eyes in white.

2 If you are going to add the toadstool, make templates from the patterns on page 124. Trace and cut out the toadstool top from red felt and the base from beige felt.

How to add the circle outline

The circle is stitched in wool yarn. Position it on the center of the pillowcase front.

1 Make a circle template by drawing around an object with a diameter of about 10in. (25cm), like a plate or saucepan lid. Mark the circle outline on the front of the pillow.

2 Stitch the outer row of the circle with running stitches, then add an inner row of running stitches in a different color, and a further row of French knots in a third color. Add some running stitches on the outside of the circle and overstitch with cross stitches in a different color.

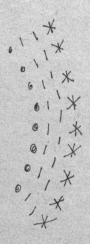

How to stitch the owl body

The owl body is stitched using embroidery floss.

1 Stitch the fly stitch feather patterning on the body following the photograph on page 77, working in rows.

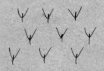

2 Stitch the running stitch feather decoration in rows on both wings in scallop shapes.

3 Stitch the beak to the owl body with yellow running stitches, and add a few seed stitches to give it texture.

4 Stitch the eyes in place, using French knots in black for the pupils and little straight stitches.

5 Pin the owl body, wings, and feet within the center of the stitched circle and stitch in place using yellow running stitches and a few stitches in brown to mark the face.

How to make the toadstool

1 Decorate the toadstool top with sequins (see page 35) attached with white running stitches and add some yellow seed stitches to the base.

2 Position the toadstool top and base to the right of the owl, and stitch them to the pillow with red running stitches for the toadstool top and yellow running stitches for the base.

Making the fox pillow

Like the owl pillow, this features a central felt fox motif, with some surrounding embroidered felt leaf motifs, a little background stitching, and an embroidered flower.

Creating the fox pillow

The fox has two templates: one for his body and head and another for his tail. You also need a template for the leaves scattered around him. The fox pillow measures 14¹/₂ x 12in. (37.5 x 30cm). The fox himself is 11in. (29cm) from tip to tail.

Things you need

- Templates on page 124
- Pillowcase in plain wool, 16in. (40cm) square
- Masking tape
- Fabric marking pen
- Small piece of orange and white felt for the fox and green for the leaves
- Anchor Tapestry wool yarn in blue, green, red, and dark red
- Anchor Pearl Cotton embroidery floss in yellow, rust, dark brown, black, green, and blue
- Embroidery needle and scissors
- Tapestry needle

Where to find

Look for plain pillowcases in homeware stores or cut up an old blanket to make your own (see page 94).

Before you start

1 Use strips of masking tape to mark out the positions of the vertical rows of running stitches, spacing them at regular intervals across the pillowcase front. Use a fabric marking pen to draw in the lines of the tape, and then remove the tape.

2 Make a template from the fox pattern on page 124. Trace around the fox template onto a piece of orange felt and cut out. Trace around the tail tip onto white felt and cut out.

3 If you are going to add the leaves, make templates from the patterns on page 124. Trace around the templates and cut out leaves from green felt.

How to stitch the background

Following the marked lines, stitch the rows in wool yarn with running stitch.

How to stitch the fox

1 Using the photograph on page 80 as a guide, stitch the pattern on the fox's back in brown fly stitch.

2 Stitch the pattern on the fox's tail in rows of yellow and brown running stitch. Stitch the pattern on the tip of the tail in white running stitch.

3 Stitch the fox's eyes, nose, mouth, and whiskers in black using straight stitches, running stitch, and backstitch to create the shapes.

4 Stitch the fox's chest in yellow seed stitches.

5 Pin the fox body and tail to the center of the pillowcase front and stitch in place with outline running stitches in orange. Do the same for the tail tip using white stitches.

How to stitch the leaves

1 Stitch the central pattern of the leaf rib in running stitch in light green on each leaf shape.

2 Pin the leaf shapes to the pillowcase front surrounding the fox as shown and stitch to the pillow with outline running stitches in light green.

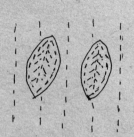

How to stitch the flower

1 Mark the outline of the flower head near the fox's head, and then work single lazy daisy stitches in red for the central part of the flower. Work them in dark red for the outer petals.

2 Mark the stem position of the flower and work two rows of green running stitch.

Other ideas

p 24
Replace the fox and leaves with the fawn and flower garden design.

Strawberry slippers

The little stitched strawberries, made from red felt, look great decorating a pair of simple cream knitted slippers but they would look equally as good decorating the pocket on a jacket, for example.

To make the stitched strawberries

You will need to cut out two strawberries in red felt using the template on page 122, reversing the template to get a matching pair. Decorate the center of the strawberry first before stitching with running stitches to the slipper. Then add the hulls for the strawberries in green wool yarn.

Things you need

- Template on page 122
- Pair of plain textile slippers
- Small piece of red felt
- Anchor Pearl Cotton embroidery floss in red, turquoise, and yellow
- Anchor Tapestry wool in green
- Embroidery needle and scissors
- Tapestry needle

Where to find

Choose a pair of plain slippers with generous textile uppers (fabric or knit) so that you can get your hand in easily to stitch onto them. Find them online, in thrift stores, or in any good department store.

Before you start

Make a template from the pattern on page 122. Trace around the template onto a piece of red felt, then reverse the template and trace out a matching one. Cut out the strawberries.

How to stitch the strawberry motifs

1 Embroider the decoration in the center of each strawberry first, making a few rows of little single daisy stitches in turquoise.

2 Make a small stitch in yellow at the other end of each single daisy stitch and add some red seed stitches inbetween the daisy stitches.

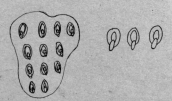

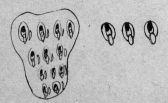

How to attach the strawberry

1 Position the strawberry motif on the slipper upper and pin in place. Then stitch small running stitches in red just inside the outline of the motif.

2 Work a few single daisy stitches in green wool at the top of each strawberry, for the green hull.

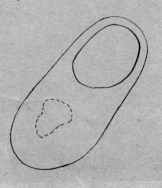

Other ideas

p 80 Use the toadstool design instead of the strawberries.

p 96 Or use the cherries design.

Needlecase

Once you've caught the sewing bug you'll find that you've collected quite a few pieces of sewing kit. A needlecase is essential for storing all your embroidery and sewing needles, together with loose pins and safety pins. Add your initials or customize it with a fun design to practice your sewing skills.

Making the needlecase design

Cut out the outer cover and a smaller rectangle for the inside from felt. The fun part comes with embellishing the cover with your choice of stitches, patterns, or motifs. Then simply sew the layers together along the "spine."

Things you need

- Piece of felt for the cover
- Piece of felt for the inside
- 3 pieces of felt in different colors for decoration
- Scissors or pinking shears
- Fabric marking pen
- Anchor Pearl Cotton embroidery floss in different colors, I used: purple, red, and mauve
- Sequins
- Embroidery needle

Before you start

1 Cut out one felt rectangle, 3½ x 6½in. (9 x 6cm) for the cover. Cut another rectangle about ¼in. (5mm) smaller all round, from contrasting colored felt, for the inside—you could cut this with pinking shears for a pretty edge, if you like.

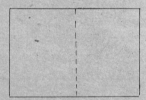

2 On three different colors of felt, mark out and cut out a circle, each one a little smaller than the last. You can use buttons to draw around.

3 On the smallest piece of felt, cut five little "v" notches, as shown.

How to stitch the needlecase

1 Position the circles on the front (largest at the base). Stitch to the case with a running stitch on each bar of the top circle. Sew a sequin in the center (see page 35).

2 Use running stitch around the outside of the largest circle in a contrasting color to attach it to the cover.

3 Place the finished cover right side down on the table and then position the smaller rectangle on top, making sure that there is an even border on all sides.

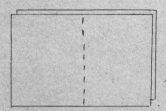

4 If you like, you could cut another piece of felt the same size as the front cover and stitch it to the inside with running stitches. The inside cover will conceal the back of your stitches used for the decoration.

How to stitch the inside of the case

Fold the needlecase in half to find the center of the smaller rectangle and mark this with a pin or draw in the center fold with a fabric marking pen. Stitch all the layers together down the center fold (the "spine") with a few backstitches.

Other ideas

Decorate a needlecase with the little flower garden from the Fawn T-shirt (see page 24) or sew a large embroidered button (see page 36) to the front.

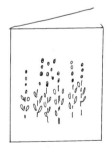 

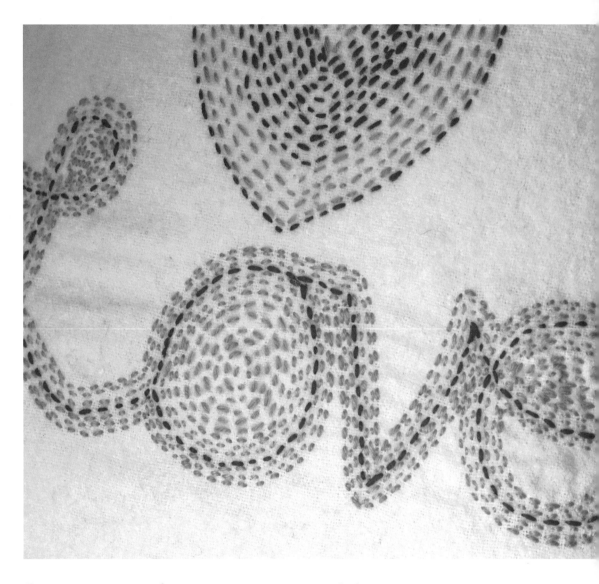

Love heart pillow

Say it with words! This cozy pillow is stitched in soft wool yarn on fabric from a recycled blanket. It's perfect for scattering in your bedroom for lazy afternoons and you can easily change the lettering to a different message or your name, or your pet's name, or just stitch the heart in your favorite colors.

Making the love heart pillow design

This very simple design is worked in wool yarns, which makes it quick and easy to stitch. You could change the word "love" to your initials if you preferred. Use your own handwriting for the words or initials to give it a nice personal touch.

Things you need

- Template on page 123
- A plain wool pillow (this one measures 16in./40cm square) or wool fabric to make pillow plus pillow form
- Fabric marking pen
- Anchor Tapestry wool yarn in 3 colors, I used: blue, pink, and red
- Tapestry needle and scissors

Where to find

You can often buy plain pillows but if you can't find one you like, it would be very easy to make one from two squares of plain fabric (I cut up old wool blankets!), stitched around on three sides. Do your embroidery before sewing the seams and inserting the pillow form, then slip stitching the fourth side to close it.

Before you start

1 Make a template from the pattern on page 123. Trace around the heart template onto the front of your pillow fabric.

2 Make a template for the lettering in your own writing to the size required for the pillow and transfer it to the pillow front, positioning it below the heart, or simply write on the fabric with a fabric marking pen.

How to stitch the lettering

1 Stitch the letters in running stitch in one color.

2 Work a couple of rows either side of the letters in the two contrasting colors.

3 Add the outline rows in a third color and fill in the circular and semicircular shapes of the "o" and "e" using rows of running stitches in the third color.

How to stitch the heart

1 Stitch around the heart outline in running stitch in one color of wool yarn.

2 Make four more rows of running stitches in a contrasting color.

3 Fill in the remainder of the heart in rows of running stitches in the first color.

Cherries dish towel

Chores are much more fun with a pretty dish towel! This cherry design will give your kitchen an injection of kitsch and would make a great gift for your Mom, too—you could even make her a matching apron (see page 72).

(see page 72)

Making the cherries dish towel design

Use a store-bought plain dish towel and add as much or as little stitch decoration as you like with some vibrantly colored threads. You can use the cherry design here, or the strawberry or cupcake motifs on pages 84 and 72 would look good, too.

Things you need

- Paper for template and a round object, like a plate to draw around, approx 5in. (13cm) diameter
- Stitch guide on page 125
- Fabric marking pen
- Plain dish towel
- Anchor Pearl Cotton embroidery floss in different colors, I used: red: dark red, green, dark green, turquoise, and pink
- Embroidery needle and scissors

Where to find

You can use an existing dish towel or pick up packs of plain dish towels in homeware stores for very little.

Before you start

1 Make a paper circle template by drawing around something with a diameter of about 5in. (13cm)—a small plate or saucepan lid work well. Position the template on the dish towel and mark the circle.

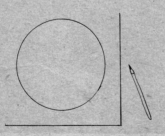

2 Make a template from the guide on page 125. Transfer the cherry motif inside the circle.

How to stitch the cherries

1 Stitch a line of running stitches around the circle in one color and then add two more rows of stitches in another color. Then work pairs of loop stiches (the first part of a single daisy stitch, see page 19) around the outer edge.

2 Next, fill in the loops with a single stitch in the center of each.

3 Outline each cherry with spaced backstitch or running stitch. Then fill in the cherries with lots of cross stitches.

4 Use running stitch and backstitch in two different colors to add the stalk and outline the leaves.

5 Fill in the veins of the leaves with running stitches in another color.

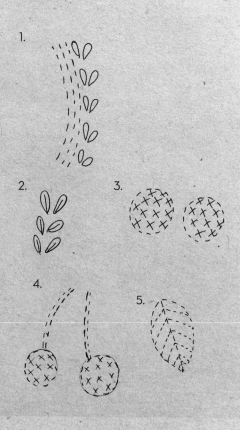

How to stitch the border

1 For a pretty finishing touch, stitch a line of running stitch right around the edge of the whole dish towel, then repeat with a second line in a different color.

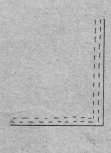

Other ideas

p 72 Use the cupcake design instead of the cherries but scale it down 20 percent.

p 84 Or use the strawberries design, using a couple of strawberries in the circle.

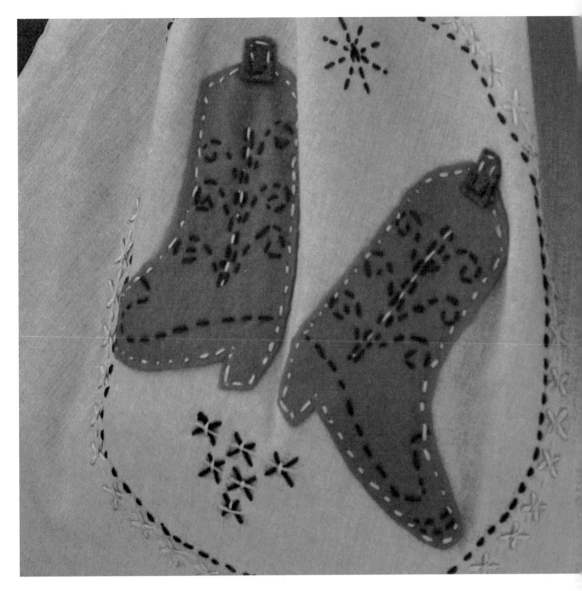

Drawstring boot bag

This pretty drawstring bag has a similar style of decoration to the shoe bag on page 44, but this time it has the addition of your initials. You could, if you wish, swap the boots for shoes and vice versa, the way you make the motif is similar in each case.

Making the boot bag design

Cut out the pair of boots from felt and decorate them with stitches before applying them to the bag. Then complete the stitched decoration on the bag: the stitched circle with a running stitch star and little rows of cross stitches. Next, add the running stitch initials and a row of combined cross stitches and running stitches at the top.

Things you need

- Template on page 125
- Paper for template and a round object, like a plate, to draw around, approx 8in. (20cm) diameter
- A drawstring bag (approx 17 x 14½in./42.5 x 37.5cm)
- Piece of orange felt, 7 x 5in. (18 x 13cm)
- Two scraps of brown felt
- Fabric marking pen
- Anchor Pearl Cotton embroidery floss in 5 colors, I used: dark red, red, blue, turquoise and yellow
- Embroidery needle and scissors

Where to find

You can use an existing drawstring bag or look for a plain one in craft or haberdashery stores.

Before you start

Make a template from the pattern on page 125. Trace around the template onto a piece of orange felt, then reverse the template and trace out a matching one. Cut out the boots. Cut out two tabs from brown felt.

How to stitch the boots

1 Using the photograph on page 100 as a guide, stitch the pattern onto each boot using the dark red embroidery floss in running stitch, remembering to turn one boot to face the opposite direction.

2 Position and pin each boot to the center of the bag (insert some card inside the bag so that you don't stitch through to the back). Then stitch around the outline of each boot and the center line of the pattern, in yellow running stitch to secure it to the bag.

3 Stitch the little tabs of brown felt to the top of each boot with running stitches in the two colors used on the boots.

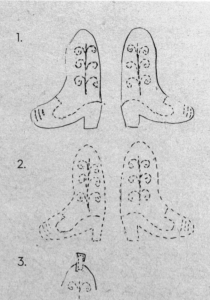

How to add the other decoration

1 Make a tracing paper circle template and mark and stitch a circle around the boots (see page 47), with two rows of running stitches, each in a different color. Work cross stitches in a third color over the outside row.

2 Mark and stitch a running stitch star to the top, working four rows of diagonal running stitches.

3 Add three rows of running and cross stitches in three colors, below the boots.

4 If you like, stitch your initials above the circle. You can draw them on as a guide or stitch them freehand in your choice of stitches.

For Giving to Friends

Why not make a special gift even more special with a hand-stitched card, gift tag, or wrapping ribbon? Here are a few ideas for hand-stitched motifs, initials, and little messages.

Cards

Gift tags

Ribbons & wrapping

Peace dove card

This pretty design makes a great motif for a card. This design works well on a piece of white linen fabric on a larger piece of patterned fabric, attached to a dark blue card. You can make your own card, but check that your design fits neatly onto the front when the card is folded. This one fits a letter size sheet folded in half, so the card fits into a standard envelope.

Making the peace dove card

Simply embroider the motif on a piece of plain linen and mount it on another piece of fabric, then your card. You can adapt this idea for any of the motifs in the book.

Things you need

- Template on page 125
- Fabric marking pen
- White linen fabric, about 4¼ x 6in. (11 x 15cm)
- Patterned fabric, such as gingham, about 5½ x 7½in. (14 x 19cm)
- Anchor Pearl Cotton embroidery floss in mid-blue
- Double-sided tape
- Plain blue card (letter size)
- Embroidery needle and scissors

Where to find

Get your card from an art supply store. You can cut your fabric down from thrift store finds, use leftover scraps, or buy it from a craft store.

Before you start

Make a template from the pattern on page 125. Trace around the template onto the piece of white fabric using a fabric marking pen.

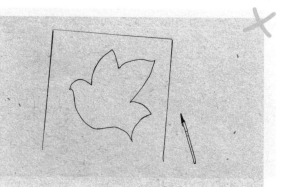

How to stitch the dove

1 Stitch the outline of the bird using backstitch.

2 Using the photograph on page 106 as a guide, stitch the pattern on the wings, body, and tail in running stitch. Add a French knot for the eye.

3 If you like, add a row of decorative running and cross stitches below the dove to finish the design.

How to apply the fabric decoration

1 Fray the edges of your fabrics (your stitched one and the background piece) by pulling the top threads out (this looks good and is quick to do). Pull out enough to make an equal border on all four sides.

2 Using double-sided tape, place the stitched fabric onto another, slightly larger piece of patterned fabric (I chose gingham but a floral or polka dot fabric would work equally well).

3 Fold the card in half and position four pieces of double-sided tape on the card front. Ease the fabric onto it, wrong side down, positioning the top first, then each side, then the base.

1.

2.

3.

Stitched heart card

The simple heart motif can be used in so many ways and is, of course, perfect for a Valentine's Day card. Use rows of running stitches in fading colors, or try chunky wool yarn on a wool or felt background for a cozy, homey feel.

Making the stitched heart card

To show you care about a special friend, why not make a card with a heart stitched on the front? The one here is stitched with simple decorative stitches, it has two pieces of fabric: a solid cotton laid over a printed check. The finished heart is stuck to a plain card.

Things you need

- Template on page 123
- Letter size plain card and envelope
- Two kinds of fabric; one solid, one printed
- Anchor Pearl Cotton embroidery floss in 3 toning colors
- Embroidery needle and scissors
- Double-sided tape

Where to find

You can get most things you need from a craft store, but why not recycle fabrics from your old clothes or from thrift store bargains?

How to stitch the heart card

1 Cut out two rectangles of fabric, the solid fabric a little smaller than the printed one, to fit on the card. Pin the fabrics together.

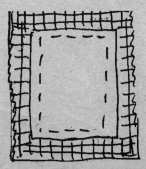

2 Make a template from the pattern on page 123. Trace around the template onto a piece of solid fabric with a fabric marking pen.

3 Using one color of thread, stitch around the outline of the heart with running stitches.

4 Stitch around again just inside this line, then add three or four more similar rows of stitching in different colors.

How to finish the card

Using fabric glue or double-sided tape, stick the stitched fabrics to the front of the card. You don't need to neaten the edges. Simply pull a few threads from each side of the rectangle to make a narrow fringe.

Other ideas

p 114   Make a matching gift tag.

p 106   Use a different motif for the card.

Gift tags

You can make really attractive yet very simple little stitched gift tags (or ribbons) to attach to any presents you want to give. It makes a lovely personal, finishing touch when giving something special to a friend.

✗ 115

Making the gift tags

You can use scraps of leftover solid and printed fabrics, card, and embroidery yarns and floss to make personalized gift tags. Here are just a couple of ideas but you can make your own versions using any of the stitch ideas in this book, or you could stitch some lengths of fabric to make ribbons.

Things you need

- Small pieces of card
- Small pieces of fabric (such as gingham, striped, or solid cotton)
- Anchor Pearl Cotton embroidery floss in matching colors
- Embroidery needle and scissors
- Double-sided tape
- Small piece of ribbon

Where to find

Buy your card from a good art supply store.
Use scraps of fabric leftover from other stitch projects.

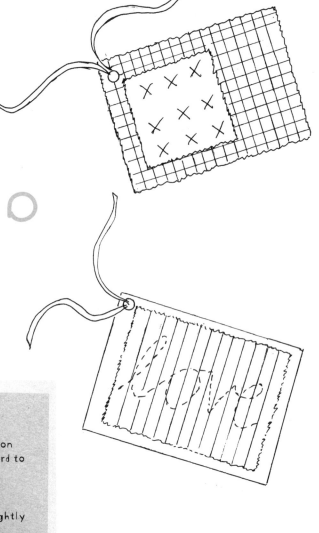

Before you start

Decide on the size of your gift tag (it will depend on what you want to stitch) and cut out a piece of card to the right size and shape.

If you are writing a message, write it out first on paper to make a template and then cut the card slightly larger than the writing.

How to stitch the cross stitch tag

1 Cut out the two fabrics, one smaller than the other, and both a bit smaller than the card you have already cut. It is not important if the edges are not completely straight.

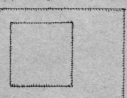

2 Stitch your chosen cross stitch pattern onto the plain fabric. When complete, stick this to the base patterned fabric with double-sided tape.

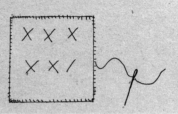

How to stitch the lettering tag

1 Transfer your lettering to the fabric.

2 Stitch the letters using simple running stitches in a contrasting color.

How to finish the tags

Fray the edges of the stitched fabrics and attach double-sided tape to the card (see page 109) and then stick the fabrics, wrong side down, onto the card, taking care to start in the center and ease the fabric out to the edges, to prevent them from wrinkling. Punch a hole in one corner of the tag and thread through some matching ribbon.

Other ideas

Make stitched ribbons from long lengths of fabric and decorate either with little stitches, such as rows of cross or running stitches, or with simple words, like "thank you" or "best wishes."

Useful Stuff

In this section you'll find all the templates for the projects.
Some are reproduced at 100 percent and others need to be
enlarged to their full size. You can also use them at any size you
choose for any of the projects or for your own ideas. There is
also a glossary giving explanations of more unusual words and
terms used in the book.

Templates

For the templates shown at 100 percent, simply trace the outline to transfer the motif to paper or card (see page 14). Some templates are shown at 50 percent of their actual size. Either enlarge them on a photocopier at 200 percent or scan them into a computer and choose your required size, then print out onto card and cut out ready to use.

Fawn T-shirt
(see pages 24–29)
100%

Phone Cozy

(see pages 40-43) 50%

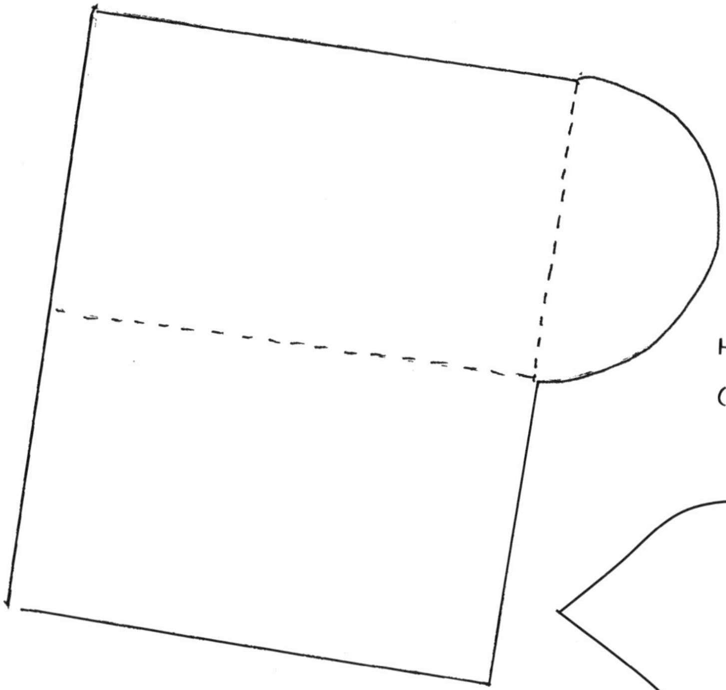

Hats & Gloves: Lips

(see pages 48-53) 100%

Hats & Gloves: XOX

(see pages 48-53) 100%

Shoe Bag (see pages
44–47) 50%

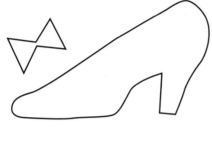

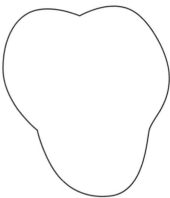

Strawberry Slippers
(see pages 84–87) 100%

Pompom Scarf
(see pages 54–57) 100%

Cupcake Apron (A)

(see pages 72–75)

50%

Love Heart Pillow (B)

(see pages 92–95)

50%

Stitched Heart Card

(C)

(see pages 110–113)

50%

A

B

C

Cupcake Apron

(see pages 72–75) 50%

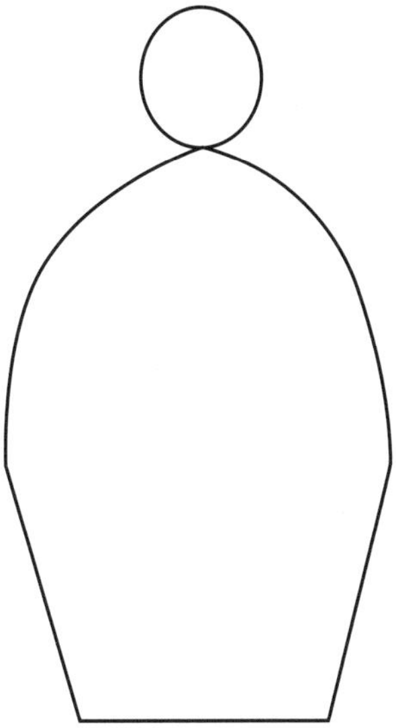

Angel Wings Top

(see pages 58–61) 50%

Owl & Fox Pillows: Owl
(see pages 76–83) 50%

Owl & Fox Pillows: Toadstool
(see pages 76–83) 100%

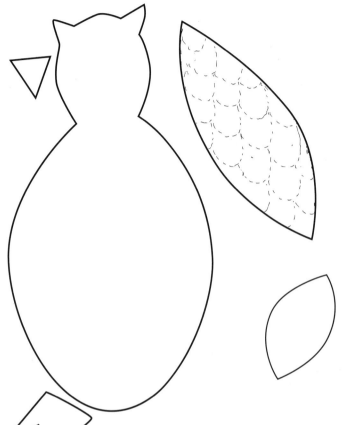

Owl & Fox Pillows: Leaves
(see pages 76–83) 50%

Owl & Fox Pillows: Fox
(see pages 76–83) 50%

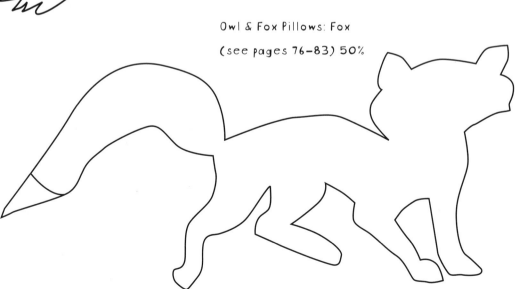

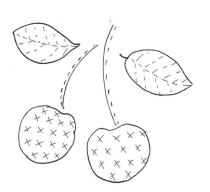

Cherries Dish Towel
(see pages 96–99) 50%

Drawstring Boot Bag
(see pages 100–103) 100%

Peace Dove Card
(see pages 106–109) 100%

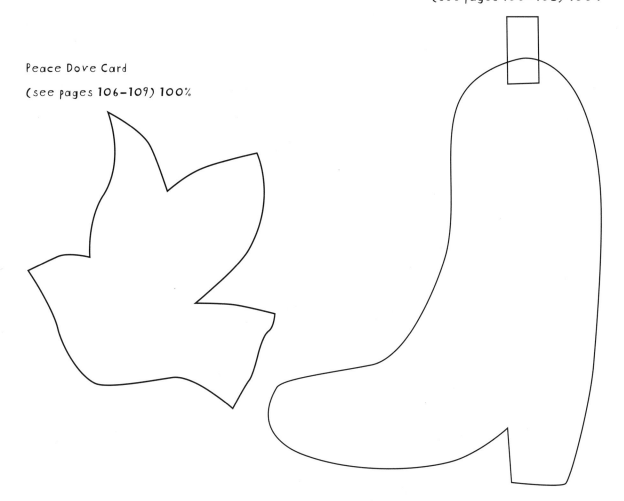

125

Glossary

Appliqué
A technique where a fabric shape is sewn to another piece of fabric.

Baste/basting
A way of holding two or more layers of fabric together temporarily by sewing long stitches, usually removed after final stitching.

Embroidery hoop
A gadget that has two hoops, one slightly smaller than the other, and a screw with which to tighten them. The fabric is inserted between the two hoops and the hoops tightened so they hold the fabric taut.

Fabric marking pen
A pen that leaves a mark that can either be removed with water or will fade away after a few days. Great for tracing templates onto fabric.

Fusible bonding web
A heat-activated fabric glue that comes on a thin sheet of paper that is ironed to the fabric and is used to attach pieces of fabric or appliqué designs securely.

Hem
The fabric that is turned up on the lower edge of a garment, sleeve or raw edge of a sewing project to provide a finished edge.

Moodboard
A collection of fabrics, stitches, yarns, and threads in different colors that you can experiment with to help you decide on color and fabric combinations.

Notch
To cut a small "V" shape into a seam or edge.

Pompom
A fluffy ball formed from wrapped strands of yarn.

Raw edge
A cut edge of fabric that has not been sewn or hemmed.

Reversing templates
You need to do this to make a mirror image of a shape, a right and a left shoe, for example.

Right side
This is the side of the fabric that will face outward, on a printed fabric it is the side with the pattern.

Seam
A stitched line formed where two pieces of material are stitched together along their edges.

Seam allowance
The amount of fabric between the edge of the fabric and the line of stitching or seam.

Sequins
Small, shiny discs with a tiny central hole that are sewn to fabric to add sparkle.

Template
A shape that you trace onto card and draw around to transfer designs to fabric.

Wrong side
This is the side of the fabric that faces inward on a project.

Acknowledgments

Author's acknowledgments

I would very much like to thank: my very patient husband, Rory Mclauchlan, who has helped with the drawings of anything from a fawn to a scarf with pompoms! He has also missed and made many meals when I was so engrossed with my book that I didn't realize the time! He constantly encourages and supports me; my daughter, Kitty Mclauchlan, who was a constant "style" adviser, answering many questions like "would you wear this?" or "could you do this?" And again, missing meals and putting up with my grumpiness! Many thanks to Susan Berry for all her help and encouragement. Finally, I'd like to thank Edinburgh College of Art for allowing me the time through my research to actually do this book.

Publishers' acknowledgments

Many thanks to all those who helped to put this book together: Steven Wooster for the photography, Shirley Mclauchlan for the illustrations, Ed Berry and Darren Brant for the original graphic concept and layouts respectively, Katie Hardwicke for editing; Polly Hardwicke, Georgie Walters, and Heloise Wooster for modeling, and Katie Hardwicke and Louisa Shulman for letting us photograph in their homes. Thanks also to Coats Crafts UK for providing the yarns and threads for the projects.

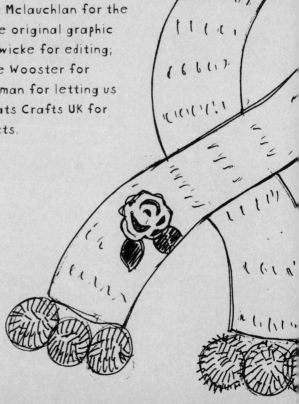